This is a Grandreams Book
This edition published in 2004

Grandreams Books Ltd, 4 North Parade, Bath BA1 1LF, UK

Designed and packaged by **Q2A Design Studio**
Printed in China

Step into the world of . . .

Knights
and Castles

Contents

The Feudal Middle Ages

Life in Europe was very different about a thousand years ago. It was a period known as the Middle Ages, a time when kings and queens reigned supreme.

The King's Noblemen

The king was the richest and most powerful man in his kingdom. He lived in grand style and wore royal robes and a crown that was often studded with precious gems. The king ruled over his kingdom with the help of his nobility, which consisted of lords, dukes, earls and knights.

In Shining Armour

And surely the most exciting of all the nobility were the knights in shining armour. Dressed in clothes of metal, knights were brave men who rode on battle horses and fought great wars. They were pure of heart and served their masters with complete loyalty. Yet, the life of a knight was about much more than just battling. Knights were experts at jousting and had mastered the codes of chivalry and honour.

During the Middle Ages, kings and queens wore crowns studded with precious stones and other gems

The Feudal Middle Ages

Which period in history is known as the Middle Ages?

The period between A.D. 500 and 1500 is usually referred to as the Middle Ages.

What does feudalism mean?

During the Middle Ages, people were divided into groups according to the work they did. Their work also defined their position in society. Each group served a smaller group, which was placed higher up in the social order. This system of division is called feudalism. At the top were the king and queen, who ruled the kingdom. Then came the lords and knights, who served the king. At the lowest level were the peasants, who were also known as serfs.

Kings

Lords

Knights

Peasants

In the feudal system, people were divided into social groups, each serving the one above them

How did feudalism begin?

King Charlemagne, or Charles the Great, ruled a large part of Europe during the late 8th and early 9th centuries. After his death, his lords and knights began to protect the peasants. The peasants, in turn, served the knights and lords, giving rise to the feudal system in Western Europe.

Which feudal group had the largest number of people?

The peasants formed the largest, and usually the poorest, group in feudal society. They lived in mud huts and worked as farmers, craftsmen and servants. Forced to pay taxes, the peasants had very little left for themselves.

Peasants used simple hair accessories that were not too costly

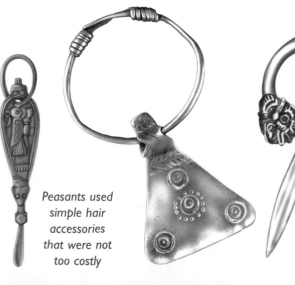

Peasants had little money left to afford jewellery after paying taxes

Many peasant families lived in very small and cramped houses

Where did peasants live?

The homes of peasants were often cold, damp and dark. Families ate, slept and spent time together in these small and cramped conditions. The houses had thatched roofs, which made them prone to fires.

Were knights also lords?

Most knights served their lords and lived as household troops. However, some knights were rewarded with lands of their own. They then became lords of the manor, with peasants serving them as farmers, workers and craftsmen. Such knights lived in manor houses and became very rich.

What did lords do, apart from owning land?

Lords made laws for the land and acted as judges to settle disputes.

What role did knights play in feudal society?

Many wars were fought during the Middle Ages and the knights were the ones who protected the king and his empire against enemies and invaders. Successful knights were usually rewarded with money or huge areas of land.

Were knights present only in Europe?

While knights were a major force in Western Europe, other countries also had such warriors. For example, in Japan there were brave warriors known as the Samurai.

A knight was a loyal subject to the king and queen

How did one become a knight?

To become a knight, one usually had to be born into a noble family. However, training to become a knight was not easy. Seven-year-old boys had to learn horse-riding and follow strict codes of conduct. At 14, they came to be called squires and learnt to use weapons and wear armour. Squires became knights only after turning 20 and, even then, they had to continue practising!

How did knights identify themselves?

While kings wore royal robes, knights too had their own unique symbols. These symbols were placed on seals, clothes, weapons and even on household articles, so that the knight could be identified.

Are there any knights these days?

Knights who fought on horseback and wore armour are all part of medieval history. However, some countries, like Britain, give knighthood to special citizens today for great service to the country. Once such a person is knighted, they are addressed as 'Sir'.

Life in the Manor House

Apart from wars, life in the Middle Ages was also about romance and a lavish lifestyle. The manor, or the castle, was the lord's home, and the person in charge of the manor was the lady. Though she had fewer rights than women today, a lady was her husband's equal in private life.

Early Marriage

A noble woman was married off by the age of 14. Her family would arrange the wedding and all her inheritance would then pass on to her husband. As a result, most knights and lords were usually on the look out to marry rich heiresses. A lady often wore expensive jewels and clothes to show off her wealth. She even wore shoes studded with gems!

The shoes of a lady or lord were often embroidered, lined with gold and crusted with precious stones

World of Charm

Ladies were largely confined to household tasks, such as weaving and spinning. However, they also hunted and fought in battles. Some learnt to use weapons to defend their homes and castles when the men were away.

Who were ladies?

A lady was the wife of a nobleman. The daughter of a duke or earl was also called a lady. The wife of a knight carried the same title too, but lost it if her husband died and she married a common man.

What was the life of a lady like?

A lady was in charge of domestic matters. She supervised officials and maids to run the kitchens and the household. She had to receive guests with courtesy and make arrangements for their stay. The lady also had servants attending to her children.

Was a lady educated?

Ladies were usually very well educated. They could read and write Latin. Some of them could even speak foreign languages!

What was the lady's main role?

Apart from looking after the household, a lady's main role in medieval society was to bear children and provide heirs for the family.

Though the lifestyles of the lady and her maid were very different they were both confined to the household

How did a lady dress?

A lady's clothes were just as expensive as the jewels she wore. She usually wore a flowing gown with a veil trailing behind. Ladies also wore elaborate and pointed hats, with long strands of pearls and other gems strung into their hairdos. Sometimes their clothes were trimmed with silver.

What kind of jewellery did a lady wear?

A rich lady wore a lot of jewels to show off her status. Gold was used the most, along with bronze and silver. Jewellery included brooches, buckles, head ornaments and rings.

Did peasant women also dress elaborately?

No, peasants were very poor and could not afford fine clothes and jewellery. Their clothes were very different from those of a lady. They wore long gowns with sleeveless tunics and wimples to cover their hair.

■ By the mid-14th century, there were laws to control who wore what jewellery. Knights were not allowed to wear rings.

Gold signet rings were also used as seals. They were usually marked with the lord's coat of arms

■ In A.D. 1149, the Order of the Hatchet was founded to honour women from Tortorosa, Spain, who had fought to stop an attack. They were excused from taxes and given more importance than men in public places.

■ Musicians also worked as clerks or teachers, but most of their income came from music, with the lord as their patron.

The lady often wore a silver-gilt brooch to pin up the top layers of her gown

What were a lord's and lady's pastimes?

When not in battle, the lord spent a lot of time with his lady. They had their own musicians, who played music to entertain their masters. Chess was another favourite pastime.

Chess pieces were often valuable. Some were carved out from ivory, while others were studded with jewels

Musicians entertained lords and ladies by playing harps and other instruments

Could women become knights?

Women could become honorary members of knights' orders, but this did not mean that they were actually knighted or that they regularly fought on battlefields. However, some women did take up arms, such as Joan of Arc in her struggle against the English in 15th-century France.

Did medieval women do any work?

Apart from household chores, women usually had to know how to spin wool. In fact, many ladies also spun woollen thread.

How did historians learn about the lives of medieval women?

Historians used tax surveys and artefacts to learn about the lives of women in the Middle Ages.

How did a lady ride a horse?

Ladies wore long gowns, which made it difficult for them to sit across a horse saddle. Instead, they rode side-saddle – with both their legs on one side of the horse.

Knights Through the Ages

D uring the Middle Ages, knights blazed through many wars, such as the Crusades, the Hundred Years War and other local battles. Over time, they acquired riches and power and it became a real honour to be a knight.

The Special Warrior

The first knights are believed to have been horse-mounted soldiers, who became prominent in England as part of King William the Conqueror's army. William was the first Norman king of England. He occupied England after the Norman conquest of A.D. 1066.

From ordinary warriors, knights gradually became a vital part of military and medieval society. Their weapons developed a lethal edge, while their armour was changed over the ages to provide greater protection from the blows of the enemy's weapons. Knights were central figures in medieval times and soon became heroes, for their legendary tales of bravery and acts of honour.

It was during the reign of William the Conqueror that the image of the knight evolved into the classical figure that we know today

How did the Holy Roman Empire collapse?

King Charlemagne conquered much of Western Europe and united it under a great empire called the Holy Roman Empire. However, his kingdom fell apart after his death in A.D. 814. Attacks by Vikings and other invaders further weakened the Empire. By the late 800s, it no longer existed.

Who were the Normans?

After the Holy Roman Empire fell, kingdoms were faced by attacks from nomadic tribes like the Magyars. To ward them off, King Charles III of France offered some land to a group of Viking invaders from the north in A.D. 911. They called their new land Normandy and came to be called the Normans.

How did the Normans come to England?

When England's King Edward died in A.D. 1066, his cousin, Duke William of Normandy, claimed the throne and attacked England with his army. He defeated the new king, Harold, in the Battle of Hastings and brought his knights and castles to the country. The Normans later moved into southern Italy and Sicily.

Charlemagne, who was considered to be a model knight, was one of the Nine Worthies – nine historical figures who symbolised chivalry

Although the Vikings fought on foot, the Normans adopted the French method of fighting on horseback

Who was the knight's enemy?

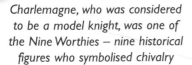

At first, knights fought Viking invaders. Viking warriors were usually foot soldiers who could not match the might of the horse-mounted knights. Later, in the Middle Ages, knights also fought other knights and gun-wielding warriors.

Why were Norman castles unique?

Norman castles were the forerunners of the later castles that were made across Europe. Norman castles were simple structures, but they introduced the method of protecting castles with built-in structures.

Why was it important for knights to own land?

A knight needed lots of money to have a good warhorse and armour. As a result, by the 1100s, most knights received some land. They used the money they got from this land to prepare for knighthood.

How did knights fight?

A knight's speeding horse could trample enemies in its charge forward. The knight could then use a long lance to injure his foes, while he stayed out of the reach of their weapons. Then, with great speed, the knight could ride off and return for another deadly attack!

FACT BOX

- The Hundred Years War began when King Edward III of England invaded France in A.D. 1337. Both the countries fought for over 100 years. The French knights were defeated several times.

- The Norman mace could deal a knock-out blow, causing broken bones or bruises!

- Making chain mail was like knitting. Its size could be changed by adding or removing the metal rings.

A medieval Norman mace

How crucial were knights to the military?

The knight became the most important warrior on the medieval battlefield. A line of charging knights with spears in hand could easily crush opposing foot soldiers. Knights were especially good in hand-to-hand combats.

Norman knights used spears like this one during battle

Were knights always a part of the nobility?

Early knights were mostly free peasants or warriors. However, as the military value of knights increased, their status rose and they became a part of the nobility. Soon, rulers and nobles began to take the title of 'knight'.

Norman knights wore knee-length mail shirts called hauberks. The hauberk was also sometimes made of cow horns

How was the knight protected on the battlefield?

Knights wore helmets and clothes of steel for protection. At first, these were made by linking metal chains together. This was called chain mail. Later, as wars became more dangerous, knights wore steel plates under their chain mail.

What kind of virtues were knights expected to have?

Knights were expected to be courteous, especially to members of their own class or those above them. They also had to be loyal to their ladies.

How did knights lose their importance?

Knights started losing importance in the 1400s. Changing military tactics and the use of guns made knights less effective.

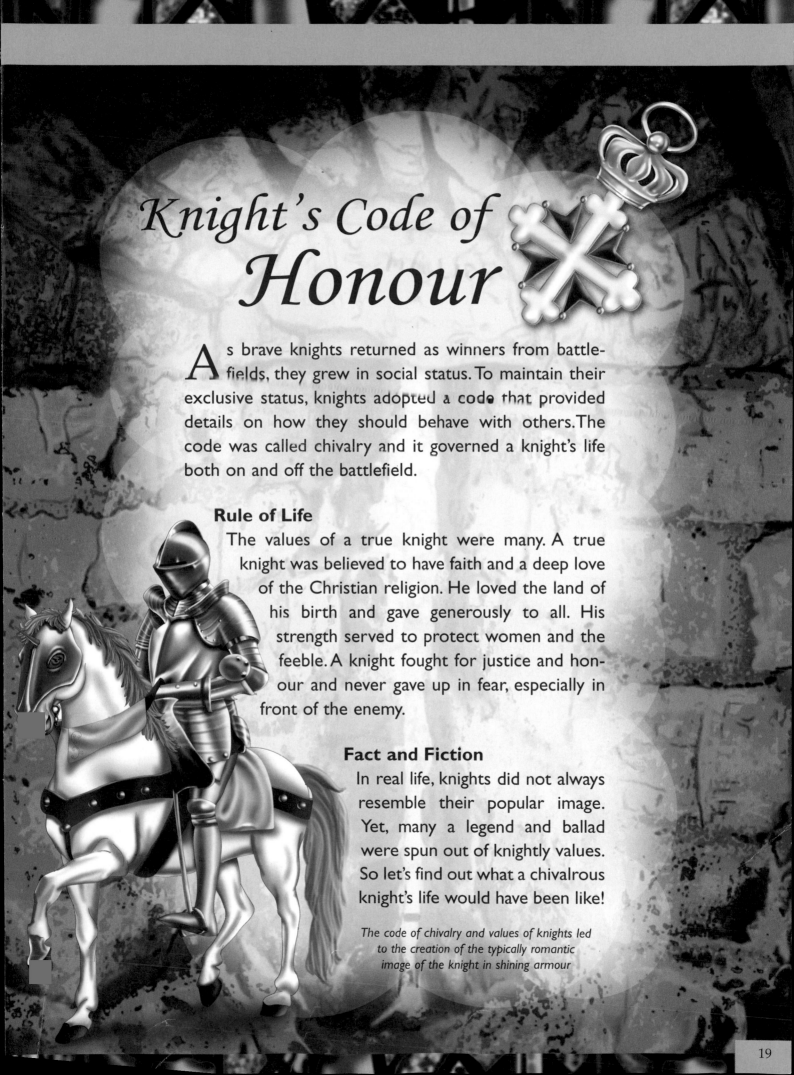

Knight's Code of *Honour*

As brave knights returned as winners from battle-fields, they grew in social status. To maintain their exclusive status, knights adopted a code that provided details on how they should behave with others. The code was called chivalry and it governed a knight's life both on and off the battlefield.

Rule of Life

The values of a true knight were many. A true knight was believed to have faith and a deep love of the Christian religion. He loved the land of his birth and gave generously to all. His strength served to protect women and the feeble. A knight fought for justice and honour and never gave up in fear, especially in front of the enemy.

Fact and Fiction

In real life, knights did not always resemble their popular image. Yet, many a legend and ballad were spun out of knightly values. So let's find out what a chivalrous knight's life would have been like!

The code of chivalry and values of knights led to the creation of the typically romantic image of the knight in shining armour

Knight's Code of Honour

What were orders of knights?

Knights formed special groups called orders. Each order vowed loyalty to their king or lord and defended his land. Some were religious orders that fought to protect Christianity, like the Templar Knights.

Knights wore badges and collars that carried the symbols and colours of the orders they belonged to

When did a knight's training begin?

A boy of about seven left home to begin training for knighthood. He joined the household of another knight, nobleman or even a king as a page. There, he learned to handle small weapons and the code of courtesy expected of him as a knight.

How did a page become a squire?

A page began his training as a squire at the age of 15 or 16 and acted as an assistant to the knight. He set the table, served meals and also received training as a mounted soldier. He rode with his master into battle. A squire's period of service usually lasted for about five years. He was then ready for knighthood.

How did knights learn the virtues required of them?

Young boys of noble birth were trained to acquire the manners they would need as knights.

How was a man knighted?

Anyone could be granted knighthood by a knight. Sometimes men were knighted on the battlefield, but the ceremony usually took place during times of peace, on the castle grounds or even in church.

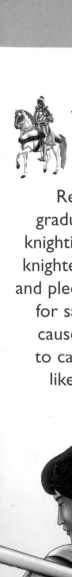

What role did religion play in the process of knighting?

Religious ceremonies gradually became a part of knighting. Before a squire was knighted, he confessed, prayed and pledged to use his weapons for sacred and honourable causes. Knights also began to carry Christian symbols like the Maltese Cross.

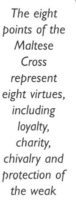

The eight points of the Maltese Cross represent eight virtues, including loyalty, charity, chivalry and protection of the weak

■ Knights' shields used images of animals and geometric shapes. Each symbol had one or a combination of seven colours – gold, silver, red, blue, black, green and purple.

What was dubbing?

Dubbing was the process by which a squire was made a knight. In a dubbing ceremony, the squire knelt before the parrain, or the man who was knighting him. The parrain struck the squire on the back of the neck, either with the palm of his hand or a sword. This was followed by the words, "I dub thee knight".

In a dubbing ceremony, the tapping of a sword on the squire's shoulders symbolised the last blows he would receive without fighting back!

■ The Order of the Garter is amongst the oldest order of knighthood in Britain.

■ A knight carried only one coat of arms. Once he died, it went to his eldest son. His other children used different versions of the coat of arms.

What is the emblem of the Order of the Garter?

The emblem of the Order of the Garter is a dark blue velvet garter edged in gold. It is worn on the left leg, below the knee.

What is the story behind the Order of the Garter?

Legend has it that while King Edward III was dancing with the Countess of Salisbury at a court ball, she lost her garter! As the king picked it up to hand it back, he saw people laughing. This made him angry and he exclaimed in French, "*Honi soit qui mal y pense*" ("Shame on him who thinks evil of it" – this became the motto of the order). He added, "I will make it so glorious that everyone would wish to wear it."

St. George is the patron saint of the Order of the Garter. This collar features a pendant depicting the famous legend of St. George slaying the dragon

How were squires granted knighthood?

At first, the knight buckled on the armour of the squire to grant him knighthood. Later, the king dubbed squires in elaborate ceremonies by touching a sword to their shoulders.

Why did knights need to have coats of arms?

When knights began to wear helmets that completely covered their faces, they could not be recognised. So, symbols were painted on knights' shields and banners to show which group they were from. As the designs became more complex, a complicated system of symbols developed. This system was called heraldry.

What is courtly love?

A knight would often worship his lady from a distance. He may never have spoken to her or seen her. Yet he would swear to protect her honour. This knightly conduct is known as courtly love.

Images of eagles lions and unicorns were popularly used on knights' shields

Weapons and Armour

A knight's main role during medieval times lay on the battlefield, where he fought many a war. A great knight was a brave man, but he needed strong armour, sharp weapons and an able horse to emerge a winner.

Hand Combat

Special care was taken in the selection of weapons for knights. Knights used a variety of weapons, like the sword, lance, poleaxe and mace. Each of these had a special use. For instance, a sword was used to cut into the enemy's body, while a mace was good for crushing bones!

In Battle Gear

All these weapons were useless, though, unless the knight had protection on his body. A knight's protective covering was called armour. It included helmets with movable visors to protect the head from heavy blows or sharp attacks. For the body, the knight wore a metallic covering, known as chain mail. Even the knight's horse wore armour when in battle!

Helmets provided protection from head injuries. This one covered the entire face, leaving slits for the eyes.

Was a knight's body armour heavy?

A full armour suit could weigh as much as 24 kg (55lb). The weight was spread all over the body to help the knight move freely. However, it did make him sweat a lot!

What kind of body protection did knights use?

Early body armour was called chain mail. It was made by connecting iron rings. Later, padded garments were worn under the mail to cushion the blows. By the 1400s, knights began to add steel plates to the armour. They also wore metal gloves called gauntlets and shoes of iron!

What kinds of helmets did knights wear?

Early knights wore conical helmets with a nose covering. These were replaced in the 1300s by stronger helmets covering the entire head.

It was difficult for a knight to put on armour on his own. The squire usually helped him out!

How crucial were swords for a knight?

A knight's sword was his most important weapon – it was the symbol of knighthood. Early knights used double-edged cutting swords. By the late 1300s, pointed swords became more popular. The sword would be carried in a leather scabbard, or case, which was attached to the knight's waist. A knight sometimes carried two swords.

What is a mace?

The steel mace was a back-up weapon for the knight. It was used if a lance had been lost or broken. A mace often had sharp spines on its head to make the blow more forceful. The handle was either made of wood or steel. Maces could crush helmets and smash bones.

What is a lance?

The lance was one of the most dangerous weapons used by knights. It usually consisted of a long wooden shaft with a sharp metal point. The speed of a charging knight on a horse made the lance deadly. He could ram the lance through the enemy's plate armour, mail and shields.

A missile or bolt from the crossbow could travel as far as 300 m (1000 feet) and pierce the armour!

■ Knights held lances under their arm, keeping them pinned against their bodies while charging at the enemy.

A metal cover on the lance protected the knight's hand during combat. This cover was called a vamplate

■ A popular thrusting sword in the late 15th century was the Italian cinqueda. It was so named because it was five fingers wide at the hilt.

■ The medieval warhorse was called a *destrier and* it usually came from France, Italy or Spain. Horses often wore decorated cloth coverings that displayed their knight's coat of arms.

What weapons did other soldiers use?

Apart from the knight, an army also had foot soldiers and warriors. Unlike the knight, they used long distance weapons, like crossbows, catapults and cannons.

What were the knight's main weapons?

The lance was the knight's main weapon, but he also used swords, maces and poleaxes. A sword hung on his left side and a dagger on his right.

The flail is a type of mace that has an iron ball attached to it by a chain. Flails were used by knights on foot

Did the knight also fight on foot?

Knights usually fought on horseback, but they also fought on foot if their horse was injured or the ground was uneven.

At royal coronations, it was tradition for a noble to hurl his gauntlet to the ground and defy anyone who questioned the king's or queen's right to rule.

How was a knight's hand protected?

Knights wore metal gloves called gauntlets on their hands These provided plate armour protection only on the outside of the hand. The knight wore leather gloves underneath to grip the weapons.

Why did knights use daggers?

As warriors began wearing armour made of plates, knights would often also carry a shorter sword, or a dagger. The dagger was easier to slip in between an enemy's plate armour at close range.

Did knights' horses also have armour?

A warhorse was costly, so knights made sure that their horses had some protection too. The horse's armour was designed to protect its rear side, neck, back and face. It was also made to wear iron horseshoes. Horse armour was costly, however, and all knights could not afford it.

The Crusades

The knights fought many famous battles during the Middle Ages, but the most well known amongst them were the Crusades. These were battles between Christians and Muslims, over the control of Jerusalem and other Eastern holy places. The knights were organised into special groups for the Crusades, like the Knights Templar and the Knights Hospitaller.

Battle Cry

The Crusades began in A.D. 1071 as the Seljuk Turks took control of Jerusalem. Pope Urban II then urged Christians to take back the Holy Land. His speech had a strong effect on everyone who heard it — clergymen, knights and the common people. "God wills it!" became their battle cry.

The Crusades lasted from A.D. 1095 to 1291. As many as eight major crusades and two children's crusades took place. Only the first and third crusades were successful. In the long history of the Crusades, thousands of knights, soldiers, merchants and peasants lost their lives on the march or in battle.

A Templar sword depicting the cross of the Templar knights

The Crusades

When was the first crusade?

The first true crusade began in August 1096. Huge armies of knights and princes took part in it and were victorious. They also set up feudal structures in the areas that were captured.

Why were more crusades fought?

Though the first crusade was a success, the winners could not hold on to the Holy Land for long. As a result, more crusades were fought for greater control.

Hospitaller knights wore black robes marked with a white cross. Meanwhile, Templar knights wore white robes with a red cross

Who were the Knights Hospitaller?

A group of monks who helped the sick turned into a military order called the Knights Hospitaller, or the Knights of St. John. Apart from battling, the Hospitallers continued to treat the sick.

Who were the Knights Templar?

The group of knights who protected Christian pilgrims in the Holy Land of Jerusalem were known as the Knights Templar. This was a religious order, but it was different from ordinary ranks of monks, as it consisted of only warriors, who fought Muslims in the Holy Land.

Did crusaders also build castles?

Crusaders built stone castles, which were heavily protected by walls. One of the most well known crusader castles is the Krak des Chevaliers in Syria. It was built by the Knights Hospitaller.

The Krak des Chevaliers is the most well preserved crusader castle

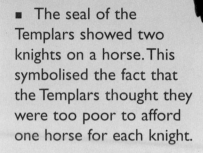

FACT BOX

- The seal of the Templars showed two knights on a horse. This symbolised the fact that the Templars thought they were too poor to afford one horse for each knight.

A Templar seal showing the famous symbol of the order

- The Knights Hospitaller continue today as an honorary organisation in Paris, France.

- There were two routes to the Holy Land from Europe. One was across the Mediterranean Sea. The other, by road, was dangerous and many knights lost their lives on the way.

What role did knights play in the Crusades?

Knights were amongst the leaders of the Crusades. They formed special groups in the name of Christ, like the Templars and the Hospitaller.

Why did the Templars cease to exist?

Over 150 years after they were formed, the Templars stopped working around A.D. 1291, when the Christians lost the Holy Land. Most Templars fell out of favour with the kings. King Philip IV wanted to seize their wealth and cracked down on the order. Many Templars stood trial or were killed and the order was suppressed.

*The shields of the three orders of Crusader knights –
Hospitaller, Templar and Teutonic*

Were Templar Knights rich?

At first, the Templars took holy vows and led a simple life. However, grants and rewards from kings soon made them very wealthy and powerful.

What was the main role of the Hospitaller Knights?

The order of the Knights Hospitaller was set up to operate hospitals, help pilgrims and spread Christianity. They were also called the Knights of Malta.

How were the Templars different from other knights?

Templars dressed differently from other knights. They wore a white surcoat with a red cross over their armour.

Who were Saracens?

Saracens were Muslims, who invaded and occupied parts of the Holy Land. They used fast horses and attacked the crusaders with arrows.

A Saracen warrior poised to attack

What was the Children's Crusade?

The spirit of holy war affected children as well as adults. Two separate groups of children set out to free the Holy Land. A French shepherd boy named Stephen and a German boy named Nicholas led 50,000 children in these crusades. Many died, while some returned home or were taken by slave traders.

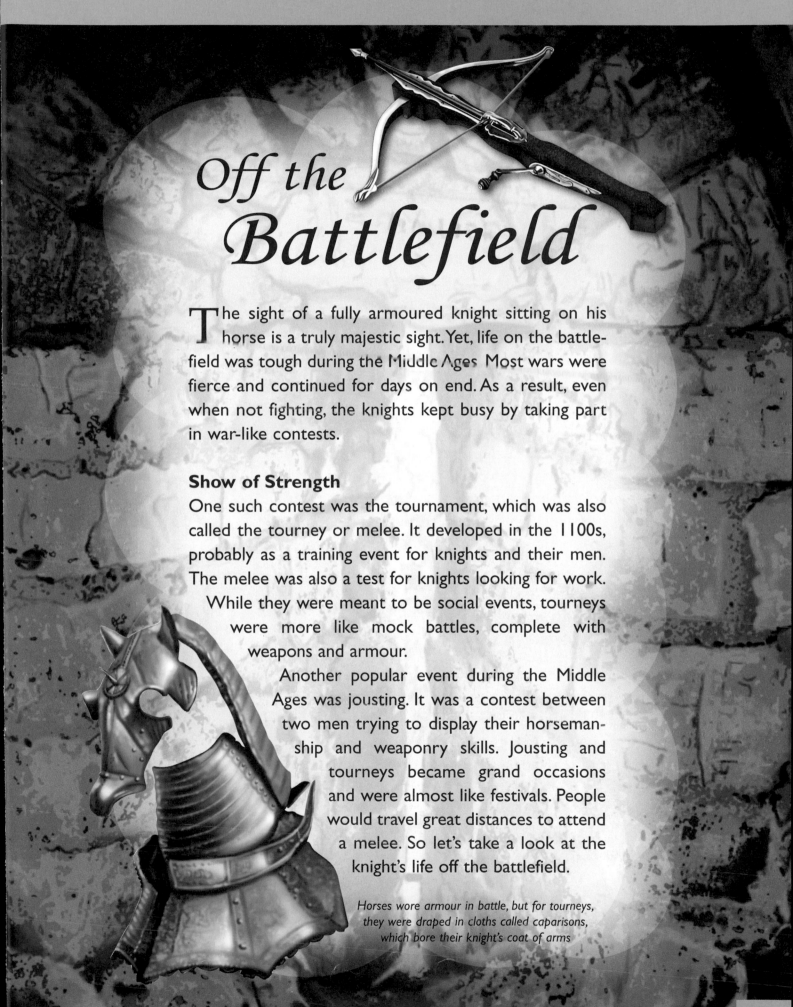

Off the Battlefield

The sight of a fully armoured knight sitting on his horse is a truly majestic sight. Yet, life on the battlefield was tough during the Middle Ages Most wars were fierce and continued for days on end. As a result, even when not fighting, the knights kept busy by taking part in war-like contests.

Show of Strength

One such contest was the tournament, which was also called the tourney or melee. It developed in the 1100s, probably as a training event for knights and their men. The melee was also a test for knights looking for work. While they were meant to be social events, tourneys were more like mock battles, complete with weapons and armour.

Another popular event during the Middle Ages was jousting. It was a contest between two men trying to display their horsemanship and weaponry skills. Jousting and tourneys became grand occasions and were almost like festivals. People would travel great distances to attend a melee. So let's take a look at the knight's life off the battlefield.

Horses wore armour in battle, but for tourneys, they were draped in cloths called caparisons, which bore their knight's coat of arms

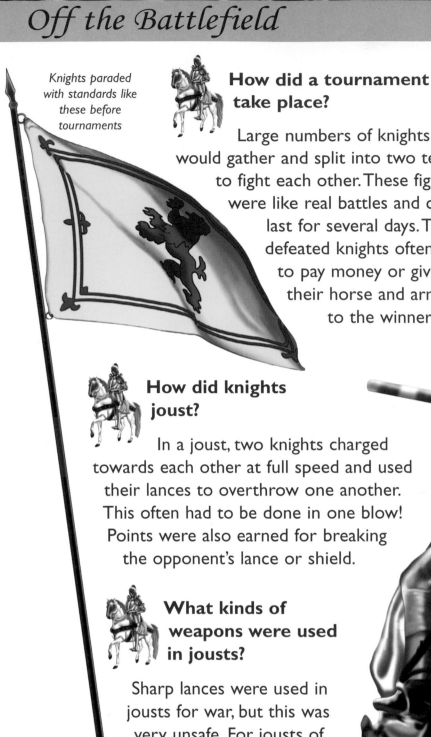

Knights paraded with standards like these before tournaments

How did a tournament take place?

Large numbers of knights would gather and split into two teams to fight each other. These fights were like real battles and could last for several days. The defeated knights often had to pay money or give up their horse and armour to the winners.

How did knights joust?

In a joust, two knights charged towards each other at full speed and used their lances to overthrow one another. This often had to be done in one blow! Points were also earned for breaking the opponent's lance or shield.

What kinds of weapons were used in jousts?

Sharp lances were used in jousts for war, but this was very unsafe. For jousts of peace, the lances were blunted or fitted with crowns at the tip. Later, shields were also used for greater safety.

When was jousting introduced?

Jousting began as an element of the tourney in the 1300s. In this event, knights fought one-on-one and showed off their special fighting skills. The aim of the game was to throw one's opponent off his horse.

Were tournaments dangerous?

At first, real weapons and armour were used at the tournaments. As a result, many knights were killed in these events. In fact, the Church wanted to ban the contests and refused to bury those killed in tournaments.

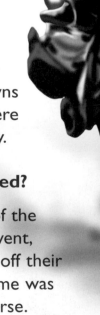

Were tourneys ever banned?

Tourneys were not banned, but by the 1300s, they became less dangerous. Special arms were made for the event, such as the blunt-tipped lance. The fighter also wore special armour that was often designed to break apart!

What was tilting?

Tilting was another popular event in the Middle Ages. Here, two knights on horseback charged at each other in narrow lanes, separated by rails to keep the horses apart. Each tried to unseat the other with a blunt lance or pointless sword. The first knight to fall off was the loser.

Unlike tournaments, jousting was about individual skills.

FACT BOX

- England's King Richard I introduced a licensing system for tournaments, which would allow them to be legally held at five sites in England.

- At one tourney held in Cologne, Germany, more than 60 knights were killed. The tourneys saw men and animals fighting in full battle gear.

- Jousts were also held on water, with opponents charging on boats instead of horses! Jousts on foot were contested with swords.

Knights wore spurs like these on their feet to urge their horses on during tourneys and jousts

Off the Battlefield

Are tournaments still held?

Tournaments became grand social events in the later part of the Middle Ages. However, by the 1600s, they was replaced by carousels. These were peaceful events exhibiting skilfull horsemanship.

Why did knights and ladies keep hawks?

Most ladies and knights had their own hawk or falcon to take part in hawking contests. The hawk was trained to fly into the air and attack game birds.

Were knights also hunters?

Hunting was a pastime for most nobles, including knights and ladies. It was a test of their courage, as they faced wild animals. Popular game animals included deer, boars, rabbits and birds.

How did the knight hunt?

Hunting was usually done in groups, with the ladies also joining in. The hunting party, accompanied by hunting dogs, used weapons like crossbows and swords.

Some lords are believed to have kept hawks in their private compartments

Did a knight's life only revolve around weapons?

Knights were not only known for their weapons. They were also famous for the lavish banquets they threw to show off their wealth and grandeur. The mounted soldiers were also famous for their many romantic relationships!

Crossbows were not only used on battlefields, but also during hunting

Fighting
from Castles

A knight's strategy in war was that of attack. And his only defensive move was retreating to the castle. A castle was not only the residence of the king or knight. It was also a fort that could ward off the enemy.

Military Role

The primary role of a castle was military. An enemy won the battle if he managed to capture the castle. As a result, castles had many special features, such as arrow slits in the walls, an iron gate called the portcullis, drawbridges and watchtowers. Each of these had a special role to play in defending the castle. For instance, soldiers could monitor the enemy's movements from the watchtowers.

Testing Time

A castle in times of peace was a place to keep armour, a treasure house and the centre of the local government. However, a castle was truly put to test during a siege. With a battery of weapons hurled at them, those at the castle had to think fast to protect themselves!

Castle watchtowers, or turrets, played a vital role in defending castles

Fighting from Castles

Behind each arrow slit was a wide bay, in which two defenders worked side by side. One loaded crossbows, while the other fired the weapons.

What was the first set of defences at a castle?

A castle usually had a ditch all around it, filled with water or stakes. This slowed down the enemy from entering the grounds. A drawbridge over the ditch, which led to the entrance, was lifted keep enemies out. The thick walls of the castle also had arrow slits for archers to shoot from.

What were battlements used for?

Battlements were platforms on top of the outer walls of the castle. These platforms projected outwards, over the walls, and stones or boiling liquids could be dropped on attackers through holes in the floors!

Did a castle's location make any difference to its safety?

Castles built on open plains were the easiest to attack. As a result, castles were soon being built on rocky crags, mountain highs or river forks. This made it more difficult for the enemy to attack.

Which was the strongest part of the castle?

The donjon, or keep, was the strongest part of the castle. It was a high, tower-like structure with thick walls at the centre of the castle. The keep could be easily defended even if the rest of the castle was captured or destroyed.

Who lived in the keep?

The lord and his family lived on the upper floor of the keep. The servants and a troop of soldiers usually lived on the first floor. The basement of the castle contained wells and storage space.

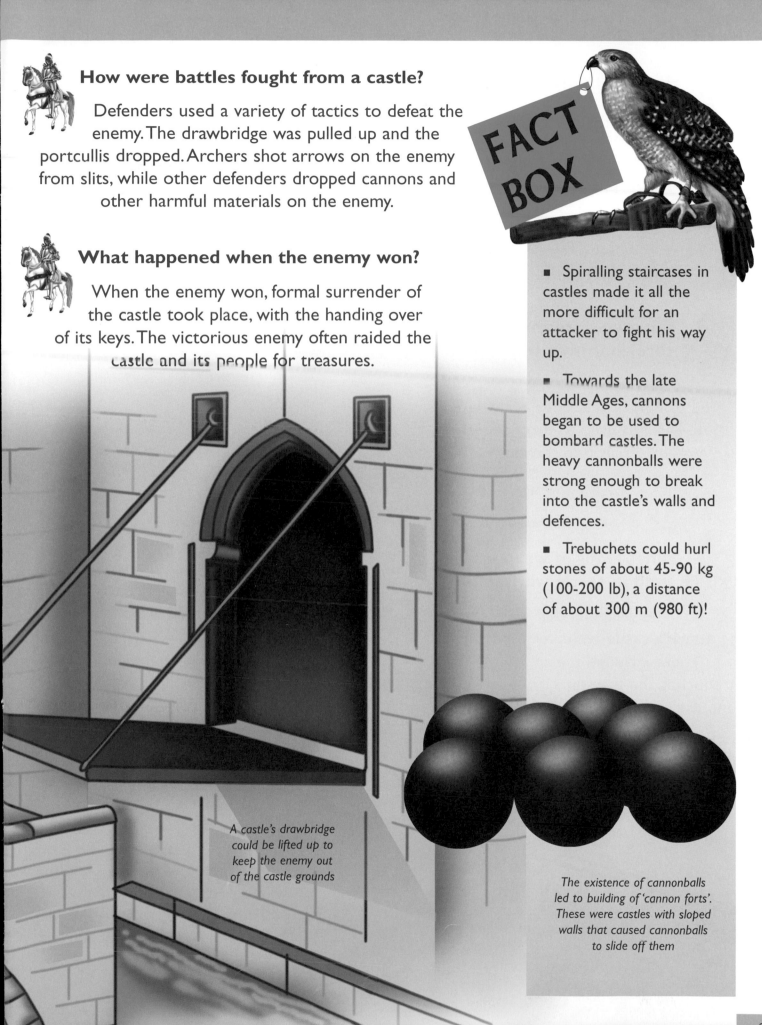

How were battles fought from a castle?

Defenders used a variety of tactics to defeat the enemy. The drawbridge was pulled up and the portcullis dropped. Archers shot arrows on the enemy from slits, while other defenders dropped cannons and other harmful materials on the enemy.

What happened when the enemy won?

When the enemy won, formal surrender of the castle took place, with the handing over of its keys. The victorious enemy often raided the castle and its people for treasures.

FACT BOX

- Spiralling staircases in castles made it all the more difficult for an attacker to fight his way up.

- Towards the late Middle Ages, cannons began to be used to bombard castles. The heavy cannonballs were strong enough to break into the castle's walls and defences.

- Trebuchets could hurl stones of about 45-90 kg (100-200 lb), a distance of about 300 m (980 ft)!

A castle's drawbridge could be lifted up to keep the enemy out of the castle grounds

The existence of cannonballs led to building of 'cannon forts'. These were castles with sloped walls that caused cannonballs to slide off them

Fighting from Castles

How did the trebuchet work?

The trebuchet worked somewhat like a seesaw. One end of the trebuchet was a sling containing a missile or stone. Dropped on the other end of the weapon was a very heavy weight, which caused the sling to fly up. This would launch the missile into the air and towards the castle.

What kinds of things were thrown from a trebuchet?

The trebuchet was a weapon used to hurl huge stones at castle walls. It was also used to drop offensive materials into the castle.

A siege tower, or belfry, was taller than castle walls. Soldiers hid in the platforms of the tower till they were close enoough to jump into the castle

What kinds of weapons were used in castle warfare?

The weapons that were used to attack a castle were very specialised. These included the trebuchet, the ballista and the catapult.

Ballistas were also known as siege bows

What was a ballista?

A ballista worked like a heavy missile launcher. It looked like a large crossbow fastened to a mount. A ballista shot over-sized bolts at the castle. These bolts were like spears and were used mainly to attack people.

How did the enemy plan his attack?

The enemy tried to break down the wall around the castle, hitting it with cannon balls and missiles. Another way was to scale the walls using ladders. Another effective way to surprise the enemy was to use a siege tower to enter the castle.

Castles in Medieval Times

Castles were crucial to the Middle Ages, since these were the homes of knights, lords and kings. Castles evolved over time, from simple structures made of wood to highly complex fortresses.

All in One

The castle was a community in itself. Everything necessary for daily living was made or found within its massive walls or on the surrounding land. Like the knight, the mighty medieval castle grew in importance because of wars and invasions. With increasing threats of attacks from raiders, lords built castles to keep their families safe.

Symbol of War

Early castles were built of earth and timber. Gradually, stone began to be used for castles, since it was stronger and fireproof. Special structures like the portcullis, a large sliding doorway of wooden or iron grillwork, were added for greater safety. Indeed, every medieval castle tells a story of warfare, weaponry and clever battle tactics!

The Romans invented the portcullis in 208 B.C.,, but it was not used in castles until 12th century A.D.

Castles in Medieval Times

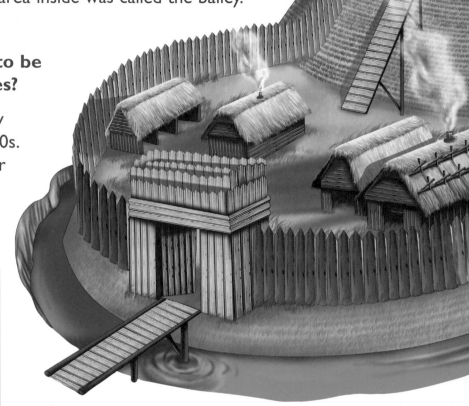

What is a motte-and-bailey?

The earliest form of the medieval castle was known as a motte-and-bailey. It was built by digging a wide circular ditch and piling earth in a huge mound. A wooden fence was made around the flattened top of the mound. The mound was called the motte and had a wooden tower on top. The area inside was called the bailey.

When did stone begin to be used for building castles?

Stone began to be widely used in castles around the 1200s. Stone walls replaced the timber fencing. These walls had square towers at first, but were soon replaced by round ones.

How did stained glass windows help to protect a castle?

Stained glass windows in castles helped to keep the residents out of sight. Stained glass often depicted battle or hunting scenes as a way of recording history.

Why were circular towers better than rectangular ones?

Rectangular towers had corners, which were easily damaged by cannons and missiles.

At first, motte-and-bailey castles were made of wood. Later, they were converted to stone

Who built the earliest medieval castles?

The Normans were the first builders of medieval castles.

What are concentric castles?

Concentric castles have two rings of wall as lines of defence. They were built so that the inner ring was higher than the outer ring. This allowed archers on the inner walls to have a clear view of the attackers.

What is special about Windsor Castle?

Windsor Castle is not a single castle, but a large complex of buildings that stretch west to east above the river. It is the residence of the British Royal Family outside of London. William the Conqueror chose the site and built the castle there in about A.D. 1070. Later kings added to the construction of the castle.

FACT BOX

- The motte was built with steep sides so that it was hard to climb. The ditch, too, was deep and difficult to cross. Sometimes it was filled with water.

- King William built castles along the borders of Wales as launching points to prevent attacks by the Welsh.

- Many castles had underground vaults called dungeons, where political prisoners or enemies of a king or noble were imprisoned. Some prisoners were kept there for life.

Windsor Castle was once the castle of the Military Knights

Prisoners were tied up inside castle dungeons with chains like these

How were the gates of castles protected?

The gates of a castle were always well protected. At Dover Castle in England, the gate was built with two huge towers on both sides. A deep, dry ditch also acted as a barrier.

Dover Castle was originally built as a ringwork castle, which was a variant of the motte-and-bailey style

What did castle keeps contain?

The keep contained a hall where people ate, kitchens where food was prepared, a chapel, toilets and places to sleep. A nobleman's family, his staff and members of their families usually lived in the castle keep.

Why did castles have windows?

Windows on castle walls were built according to a battle plan. The lowest windows of the towers were fairly high off the ground and very narrow. This was so that archers could fire accurately from inside. Higher windows and those in the inner buildings were larger, to let in light. They were often fitted with clear or stained glass.

Why did castles decline in importance?

Medieval castles were not well protected from gunfire. As they began to lose their military significance, they began to be used only as residences. As a result, castles became more decorative and lavish.

Did keeps also change over time?

Keeps were originally rectangular structures, between two to four stories high. The entrance to the keep was usually on the second floor. Later, keeps were built with round towers, which were easier to defend from attacks.

Castle bedrooms and living rooms contained elaborately carved fireplaces

Knights in Legends

Knighthood and chivalry have always been favourite themes in literature. Many legends and stories have been created around the lives and times of kings, knights and their ladies. There are tales of brave knights slaying dragons, of heroes performing extraordinary feats for their ladies and of men fighting for the poor.

The Greatest King

One such group of medieval stories makes up the famous Arthurian legend – the tale of King Arthur and his Knights of the Round Table, who included Sir Lancelot, Sir Galahad and Sir Gawain. These men searched for the Holy Grail, protected the weak and were guided by the love of fair ladies.

Arthur was said to be the greatest icon of kingship. He was brave, wise and powerful. He was also seen as the protector of the weak and poor. King Arthur's knights were a part of the Order of the Round Table. Each one of them was a great knight. The story of King Arthur and his knights has been included in a number of poems and stories of medieval times.

Several myths and legends depict knights as warriors who fought dragons

Who was King Arthur?

According to legend, Arthur was the son of King Uther Pendragon. Immediately after his birth, Arthur was put into the care of Merlin the Magician. Merlin took him to Sir Hector, who brought the child up as his own son.

What was the Excalibur?

The Excalibur was King Arthur's sword. Different legends explain how Arthur obtained the sword. One legend states that Excalibur was embedded in a block of stone such that only the rightful heir to the throne of England could pull it out. Many men tried to pull out the Excalibur, but only Arthur succeeded.

What is the tale of the Lady of the Lake?

According to another version of the Excalibur legend, Arthur received the sword from the mysterious Lady of the Lake. She lived in a castle at the bottom of a magic lake. Story has it that her arm appeared above the surface of the lake with the sword in hand. When Arthur took it from her, the arm disappeared!

Who lived in the castle of Camelot?

King Arthur and his queen, Guinevere, are believed to have lived in the castle of Camelot, the exact location of which remains a mystery to this day. Camelot was said to form the centre of the Arthurian world.

According to another legend, it was Sir Arthur's knight, Sir Galahad, who pulled out Excalibur

What is the tale of the Round Table?

According to legend, the Round Table was given to Arthur when he married Queen Guinevere. It was said to seat between 150 to 1500 men. The nobles who sat at the Round Table were all included in the Order of the Round Table.

Why was Sir Lancelot considered to be the most chivalrous of all knights?

It is believed that Sir Lancelot was brought up by the Lady of the Lake. She taught him the perfect art of chivalry and sent him to King Arthur's court.

Who were Sir Lancelot and Sir Galahad?

Sir Lancelot was considered to be the most chivalrous of all legendary knights. Story has it that Queen Guinevere and Sir Lancelot fell in love, leading to the break up of the Round Table and the fall of Camelot.

Sir Lancelot's romance with Queen Guinevere led to a battle between him and King Arthur. While King Arthur was away fighting Sir Lancelot, his nephew – Mordred – was left in charge of the kingdom

FACT BOX

- The term Camelot is associated with the high values displayed by King Arthur – that of a strong leader during peaceful times. The presidency of John F. Kennedy was also referred to as Camelot.

The shield of Mordred depicted a majestic unicorn

- Mordred was said to be the son of King Arthur's half-sister, Morgan, or Ann-Morgause. He is said to have been killed by Arthur in the Battle of Camlann.

- A poem on Sir Galahad says, "My strength is as the strength of ten because my heart is pure".

The Mandylion was later adopted by the Templar Knights

What was the Mandylion?

In legends and stories, Sir Galahad has always been associated with the Holy Grail. He was also linked with the Mandylion, the linen cloth that was used for wrapping the body of Jesus. The Mandylion is now known as the Shroud of Turin.

What is believed to have happened to King Arthur when he was injured?

It is believed that the injured body of King Arthur was mysteriously carried away to the Island of Avalon to be healed. He was expected to return in future and resume his rule.

The Holy Grail is bellieved to be the cup that was used by Jesus at the Last Supper

How was King Arthur injured?

King Arthur's evil nephew, Mordred, betrayed his uncle. He is even said to have kidnapped Queen Guinevere. In a great battle that followed his betrayal, Mordred was killed, but not before he wounded King Arthur.

Who succeeded in the quest for the Holy Grail?

The Holy Grail is said to be the cup used by Jesus at the Last Supper. According to legend, only the pure at heart could hold the Holy Grail. King Arthur is said to have been on a quest for the Grail. However, it was Sir Galahad who was finally successful in finding it.

Is there any truth in the stories of King Arthur?

Some scholars believe that there was an historical Arthur, who lived in Britain in the 5th or 6th century. He was defeated and killed in battle. His people fled to the mountains of Wales and Brittany in France. There they told glorified stories of Arthur's courage and good deeds.